D1414198

WALSALL
THEN & NOW
IN COLOUR

DAVID F. VODDEN

First published in 2011

The History Press
The Mill, Brimscombe Port
Stroud, Gloucestershire, GL5 2QG
www.thehistorypress.co.uk

British Library Cataloguing in Publication Data.
A catalogue record for this book is available from the British Library.

ISBN 978 0 7524 6298 1

Typesetting and origination by The History Press
Printed in India
Manufacturing managed by Jellyfish Print Solutions Ltd

CONTENTS

Acknowledgements   4

About the Author   4

Introduction   5

Walsall Then & Now   6

ACKNOWLEDGEMENTS

I would like to thank the following people for their help and encouragement and for the use of old photographs in this book:

P. Abbott, the late J. Aspinall, R.A.Brevitt, Mrs N. Hilton, Mrs N. Hobbs, the late Dr C. Hollingsworth, J.S. Hunt, B. Lowe, J. Leadbeatter, the late Prof. O. Naddermier, S.L. Parkes, D.J. Payne, A. Preston, K. Rock, Misses N. and M. Sankey, the late R.A. Stone, the late J.S. Webb, Mrs M. Ward, G.Whiston and the late Mrs P. Winton.

ABOUT THE AUTHOR

David Vodden became head of history at West Midlands College, Walsall, in 1970 and has lived in Walsall since 1972. Fascinated by local history, he is currently a member of several important societies, including the Black Country Society and Friends of Black Country Museum, as well as being vice chairman of the Civic Society and former president of Rotary and of the Walsall Photographic Society. David is an enthusiastic photographer and traveller, with a keen interest in visiting historical and archaeological sites.

INTRODUCTION

This selection of pictures is a mixture of old views and the current scene taken mainly by the author eleven years into the Millennium.

During the twentieth century there has been a tendency to demolish the town centre and neighbouring buildings periodically and to re-build. In this way, many attractive, even medieval, buildings have been lost and not all their replacements have met with widespread approval. Certainly, it was right to carry out slum clearance, but there were fine public buildings, private houses and commercial premises destroyed in the name of progress.

Several years ago, I was alerted by the late Percy Farmer to Sir John Betjeman's article in the *Telegraph* dated 24 August 1959 in which he described how he had spent a day of his holidays in Walsall: 'an ancient borough', which had

> ... once been the centre of the leather trade. The streets were wide and comparatively free of traffic. There was a rich and splendid Town Hall, an impressive Victorian church by Pearson [St Paul's] and then something quite unexpected and beautiful.
> This was an old High Street with cobbled sides and trees: inns now turned into shops or offices climbing up to the Georgian Gothic west front of the parish church. This church was on a high, grass hill which had been cleared of stumps and laid out as a grassy space with a walled garden and a seemly row of two-storey modern flats in local brick designed by a good architect.
> Walsall is a borough which is obviously proud of itself and I thought that if the local council were to turn this old High Street into something worthy of the charming and modest buildings, Georgian and Victorian, above the shop fronts it could be made into one of the most attractive streets in England.

Much of the re-development of Digbeth, Old Square and the High Street has taken place within a decade or so of Betjeman's visit and I have been fortunate in being lent pictures of the scene in the 1950s and some of the changes taking place in the 1960s, which I have matched with my own pictures of the present.

In addition to changes in the town centre I have also included pictures of places from the edge of town, such as the Mellish Road Wesleyan Church. The Grange Farm, Brookhouse Farm and Park Hall are also pictured with their modern counterpart of housing and a school.

Collecting the evidence has been most enjoyable and I hope it will provide hours of pleasure and interest for the reader.

THE HIGH STREET

THIS IS AN early view of the High Street in around 1900. The trees are young and there is no evidence of petrol-driven vehicles. Halfway up the left-hand side stands the Guildhall, which opened in the 1860s. A local architect, the late Gordon Foster, MBE, FRIBA, acquired the Guildhall when it had become derelict and restored it as a shopping precinct with office

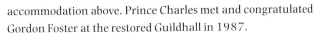

accommodation above. Prince Charles met and congratulated Gordon Foster at the restored Guildhall in 1987.

THERE IS NOT a great deal of change between this picture of the High Street now and the last except that it was taken a little further down the hill, more or less under the present Overstrand. On the left, the Green Dragon Inn has been merged with the former Bear and Ragged Staff and is currently trading as the Black Country Arms. On the right, the site of the old music hall, having boasted a Sainsbury's for a time, has undergone further redevelopment and is now home to an Asda supermarket. The market stalls have moved further down the hill and parking is allowed only to disabled drivers.

THE OLD STILL

THE OLD STILL, demolished in 1959, looking east from The Bridge.
It had stood in Digbeth since at least the eighteenth century. This view
dates from the 1930s. It is said that Dr Johnson, who lived in Lichfield,
would wait here before he caught the coach from the nearby George
Hotel on his way home from London. The licence was transferred to
The Leathern Bottle, Bloxwich in 1959.
(Reproduced with kind permission of Mrs N. Hilton)

THE CORNER OF Lower Hall Lane in Digbeth is the site of the former
Old Still and Dances' Tea Rooms. The Old Still had had stabling for
four horses. Billy Meikle, the local artist and pioneer photographer,
said of the Old Still: 'What is about to be destroyed is very old and
original... it is now without doubt the oldest pub in existence in
Walsall'. Meikle might have forgotten the medieval Woolpack or even
the White Hart, Caldmore!

THE TALBOT HOTEL

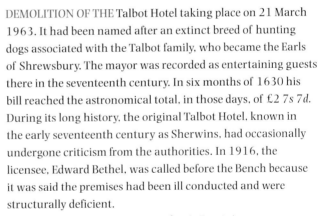

DEMOLITION OF THE Talbot Hotel taking place on 21 March 1963. It had been named after an extinct breed of hunting dogs associated with the Talbot family, who became the Earls of Shrewsbury. The mayor was recorded as entertaining guests there in the seventeenth century. In six months of 1630 his bill reached the astronomical total, in those days, of £2 7s 7d. During its long history, the original Talbot Hotel, known in the early seventeenth century as Sherwins, had occasionally undergone criticism from the authorities. In 1916, the licensee, Edward Bethel, was called before the Bench because it was said the premises had been ill conducted and were structurally deficient.

(Reproduced with kind permission of R.A. Brevitt)

THE CURRENT BUILDING was put up by Mitchells and Butlers (M & B), following the demolition of the former Talbot Hotel, Digbeth, but is now partly an amusement arcade.

THE HIGH STREET
AND DIGBETH

THE HIGH STREET as seen from the Talbot Hotel, Digbeth, in 1965. Already, the first stage of re-development had taken place. Although one can see the left-hand side of the High Street from

here and Phillips' fish shop on the right-hand side in Digbeth,
St Matthew's church is out of sight.

THE HIGH STREET and Digbeth are viewed here from the
former Talbot. This photograph is taken through the same
archway as the previous picture; this was an early part of the
re-development of Digbeth. Nowadays, most of the market has
been re-located to The Bridge, Bradford Street, and the lower
end of Park Street, but the stalls are left up all the time as there
are four market days a week.

ST MATTHEW'S CHURCH

ST MATTHEW'S CHURCH from Tantarra Street, *c.* 1960. Although terraced houses have been demolished, the school remains and has been converted to housing for the elderly by Walsall & District Housing Trust. Tantarra is thought to relate to the huntsmen's cry of 'tally ho' as they set off for the open countryside.
(Reproduced with kind permission of D.J. Payne)

ST MATTHEW'S CHURCH viewed from Tantarra Street. As with Paddock Lane, there has been demolition of housing, and the view from the middle distance to the parish church is considerably changed. In the foreground, on Ablewell Street, there is now a Lidl supermarket with a car park. New residences have been built to the left of the supermarket.

PADDOCK

PADDOCK WAS ONE of the medieval common fields and it may also have been associated with grazing for horses during the coaching era. Seen here from Church Hill in 1963, Paddock shows a densely packed mixture of housing and factories or workshops, which is probably a scene little changed from the period of increased industrialisation of the mid-nineteenth century.

THE VIEW OF Paddock from St Matthew's churchyard is much altered as the skyline is now dominated by the flats in Union Street. Much Victorian terraced housing lower down the hill has gone, although the former Tantarra Street school has been converted to retirement homes. The Lidl supermarket is in the centre foreground, and off to the right is a residential block in Tudor revival style.

THE HIGH STREET
AND MARKET

THIS 1965 PHOTOGRAPH of the High Street and market from the church is dominated by the cross of the 1922 outdoor pulpit on the left and Hillans' draper's shop on the right. The Guildhall

on the right of the High Street was used as a court until 1976. In this view the middle distance seems to be suffering from atmospheric pollution and the Reedswood Power Station isn't visible on the skyline.

(Reproduced with kind permission of D.J. Payne)

THIS IS THE High Street now, but the market has been relocated. The church still has the cross on the left, but Hillans' shop has been demolished and the site landscaped. The Guildhall has been restored as a base for a number of retail outlets. On the opposite side of the High Street there is now an Asda Supermarket, which has replaced a Sainsbury's store. In the distance can be discerned the new art gallery dominating the view at Town End.

CHURCH HILL

LOOKING DOWN CHURCH Hill *c.* 1900, on the left is a series of good Victorian houses with the Shakespeare Inn down on the corner. This cobbled street was the main route out of the High Street to the ancient parish church of St Matthew. The junction of High Street and Upper Rushall Street at the foot of this exceedingly steep slope is always regarded as the very origin, geographically, of Walsall in Saxon times. This hill was also the site of the first workhouse in the eighteenth century.

LOOKING DOWN CHURCH Hill today, the houses and the Shakespeare Inn have been demolished and the slopes landscaped. On looking through the railings near the bottom of

the hill, some doorsteps can still be spotted. Right at the bottom of the cobbled street runs the Upper Rushall Street section of the Inner Ring Road which now cuts off the parish church from the High Street.

WALSALL MEMORIAL GARDENS

HRH PRINCESS MARGARET at the Walsall Memorial Gardens where she unveiled the memorial stone, which is in the foreground covered by a Union Jack, on 1 May 1951. The gardens were

designed by G.A. Jellicoe, FRIBA, and stand partly on the site of the Leathern Bottle, which was closed in 1939. The photograph was provided by the late Mrs Pam Winton whose husband, Mr Jim Winton, was Head of Parks and Gardens for the Borough Council and can be seen next to the Chief of Police on the left of the photograph, while Mayor W.R. Wheway is at the microphone.

(Reproduced with kind permission of the Late Mrs P. Winton)

THE WALSALL MEMORIAL Gardens have recently been refurbished. The memorial stone in the gardens was carved by Gordon Hericx, lecturer in sculpture at Walsall Art College, Goodall Street. During a crowded programme that afternoon, the princess also visited the mayor's family chain-making business.

LOWER RUSHALL STREET

ST MATTHEW'S FROM Lower Rushall Street, as depicted by Vincent Murray in 1947. Although the site for the Warewell Flats on the left seems to be derelict, the Borough Arms is shown on the corner of Upper Rushall Street. On the right, Eylands' Buckle Works was still operating. Walsall Lithographic produced fifty prints of this drawing.
(Reproduced with kind permission of the late J. Aspinall)

LOWER RUSHALL STREET today has car parking on the left. The Borough Arms stands isolated in Upper Rushall Street, the other shops having been demolished in order to establish a one-way traffic system around the back to facilitate deliveries to Asda in the High Street. On the right, Eylands' Buckle Works has been restored as housing and one can still detect archways and other details from the previous picture.

CRABTREE'S

CRABTREE'S ORIGINAL WORKS was established in Upper Rushall Street, in 1919; this building has now been converted to accommodation for the Lyndon House Hotel. J.A. Crabtree came to Walsall and occupied a former leather works where he designed and manufactured

electrical switchgear. By 1926 the firm had become so successful
that it moved to new purpose-built accommodation at Beacon Street,
which site is now occupied by over sixty domestic houses recently
built by David Wilson Homes.
(Reproduced with kind permission of A. Preston)

LYNDON HOUSE HOTEL has replaced the New Royal Exchange and
taken over the building next door (Crabtree's original works). The
Bull's Head used to stand across the road where there is now a new
road junction and a car park. Considerable further expansion has
taken place to the rear of the Lyndon House Hotel, extending down to
Goodall Street where a Salvation Army hostel used to stand.

GOODALL STREET

THE MASONIC HALL, Goodall Street, seen here in 1964, was a former Baptist chapel and school dating from 1833. It was purchased in 1930 by three members of the Hatherton Lodge to serve as the Freemasons' meeting venue. On 9 December 1971 it was sold to developers, however, and it was subsequently demolished. Freemasons then initially held their Lodge meetings temporarily in Wednesbury before the present Compass Suite was completed at Aldridge in 1974, designed by local architect John N. Barratt.
(Reproduced with kind permission of R.A. Brevitt)

TAMEWAY TOWER, GOODALL Street, photographed in 1999, covers not only the Masonic Hall site but also that of the Gas Office. It was built as a speculation originally and the office space it contained took time to let. Goodall Street takes its name from a Birmingham banker, Francis Goodall, who had owned the land in the late eighteenth century on which the street was eventually laid out in the first quarter of the nineteenth century. Since the Masonic Hall was disposed of, local Freemasons' lodges now hold their meetings at The Compass Suite, Aldridge.

FREER STREET

THE EMPIRE, FREER Street, is pictured here in 1954. Formerly a Temperance Hall, it had been built by the Walsall Temperance Association to the designs of Loxton Brothers of Wednesbury in 1866, with seating for 1,000. Having been used as a place of worship by Presbyterians in 1877, and serving as a venue for a new Literary Institute, which held weekly lectures there from 1884, it was eventually to become one of six early cinemas in the borough. Now, there are none in the town centre, the nearest being in Bentley Mill Way near Junction 10 of the M6 motorway.

FREER STREET WAS named after Dr George Freer of Birmingham who became Francis Goodall's son-in-law by marrying Joanna Goodall. Debenhams now occupy the site of the Empire Cinema, with a multi-storey car park adjacent. For some years, Freer Street has been one-way for traffic but in the earlier photograph on p. 29 there is a sign pointing to a car park against the current flow of traffic.

LEICESTER SQUARE

LEICESTER SQUARE IN May 1935 with the bunting displayed for the Silver Jubilee of George V.
A new pedestrian crossing was created at the bottom of Freer Street in 1952 near the Black Swan,
known in those days as The Stork.
(Reproduced with kind permission of Mrs N. Hobbs)

THE FORMER BLACK Swan by the pedestrian crossing at the bottom of Freer Street, known for
a time as The Stork, could be traced back to at least 1845. It was renamed The Dirty Duck in the
1960s and was originally a posting house. These were established in the sixteenth century to enable
royal messengers and later post office coaches to change horses along major routes. It is situated in
Leicester Square, which itself takes its name from Queen Elizabeth I's favourite, Robert Dudley, Earl
of Leicester, who was the third son of John Dudley, Lord of the Manor of Walsall. In the background
stands the former Co-operative Store with the Kenmare Restaurant upstairs. Currently, the County
Court is housed on the first floor above a club and shops. The offices of the Co-operative Society in
Hatherton Road are about to close and the work transferred to Leamington Spa.

THE BRIDGE

A VIEW OF The Bridge before the First World War, showing the original clock (nicknamed the 'Four-faced Liar' because the individual faces did not always display identical times!)

The building on the right used to house the former *Walsall Observer*. For many years The Bridge was open to traffic, including public transport. It served as the site of the terminus for the Bloxwich trams. Currently, it is completely pedestrianised.

THE BRIDGE LOOKING north. Nowadays, part of the market has been established on the bridge. Also visible is the 'Source of Ingenuity' Fountain by Tom Lomax, which was part of a £1.8 million rejuvenating of the town centre. Regrettably, the fountain remains dry for health and safety reasons. It is based on Janus (a god from Roman mythology, usually depicted with two heads, who looked forward and backwards) and comprises a young man's face surmounted by a disc carved with tools of the town's traditional trades, such as leatherworking, while the other side has an old man's face and electronic circuit boards and other symbols of the modern age.

THE BRIDGE AND CLOCK

THE BRIDGE AND clock. This was decorated in May 1935 for George V's Silver Jubilee. The clock, the 'Four-faced Liar', stands in front of buildings which include the Odeon and the George Hotel,

which was a coaching inn. It was established by Thomas Fletcher of the Green Dragon Inn in 1781 and fronted from 1823 by pillars from Fisherwick Hall and, next door, the former Odeon cinema of which Phil Cross was manager for many years.

(Reproduced with kind permission of Mrs N. Hobbs)

THE SITE OF the former Odeon has been occupied principally for some years by a Tesco Metro superstore. This has now closed and it is planned for a Primark to be established in the building. Part of the four-day-a-week market is shown on the bridge and the lower part of Digbeth. The original clock has been replaced by one with a modern movement.

ST PAUL'S BUS STATION

THE BUS STATION, which opened in 1935, had been built at a cost of £16,378 on the site of the former Bluecoat School after the new school had been opened in Springhill Road. This shows the bus station as pictured in 1954. When it began operating, buses and trolleybuses that had previously terminated on The Bridge were re-routed here. *(Reproduced with kind permission of R.A. Brevitt)*

THE NEW ST PAUL'S bus station is in the middle distance. It was completed at the beginning of the Millenium and in plan it is oval and contains offices, waiting rooms and toilets. Peeping over the top, the clock on the roof of the former bus station building can just be seen. On the right of the picture the Midland Bank now trades as HSBC.

THE COUNTY COURT HOUSE

THE COUNTY COURT House prior the First World War, taken from a lantern slide. This building, costing 1,600 guineas, was intended for a library in 1836 and then was renamed St Matthew's Hall. Eventually, it became the County Court. More recently, it has become a restaurant, while court is now held in the former Co-operative building in Upper Bridge Street. It has recently been acquired by Wetherspoons.
(Reproduced with kind permission of D.J. Payne)

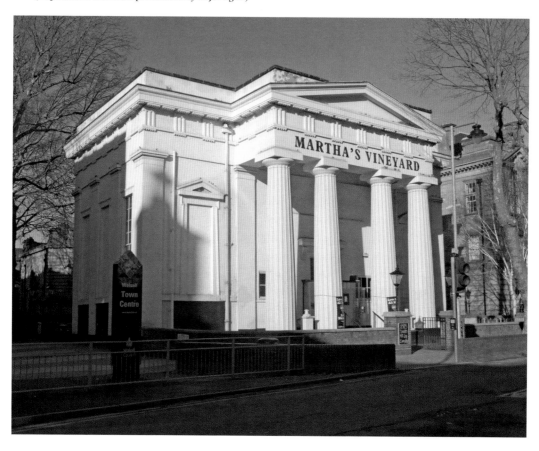

THE OLD COURT house is now a restaurant, which traded for a time as the Old Court House but has now been re-named Martha's Vineyard. Leicester Street runs down the left-hand side of the building and has now been pedestrianised, as has Darwall Street, to create a Civic Quarter. To the right stands the very early twentieth-century Council House, the foundation stone for which was laid by Queen Victoria's son-in-law, Prince Christian of Schleswig-Holstein on 29 May 1902.

THE IMPERIAL

THE IMPERIAL CINEMA is seen here as a bingo hall. It had been built originally as an agricultural hall and was then re-named St George's Hall. In 1881 it was converted to a theatre with almost 2,000 seats and then became Walsall's first cinema in 1908. Its change of function to being a bingo hall, as shown, came in 1968.

THE IMPERIAL STANDS in Darwall Street, which takes its name from the original landowner, not one of the two eighteenth-century vicars of St Matthew's parish church. The Imperial has now been converted to a public house owned by Wetherspoons. The exterior shows slight changes over the years, not least the fine lamps.

TILDESLEY'S

REGINALD TILDESLEY IN Lichfield Street in the late 1960s (note the roadside petrol pump). Lichfield Street had been built in 1831 to replace the route to Lichfield along Rushall Street and cutting across the site of the present Arboretum lake. Tildesley's moved in more recent times to Wolverhampton Street to become a Main Ford Dealer, where they advertised that they gave 'a

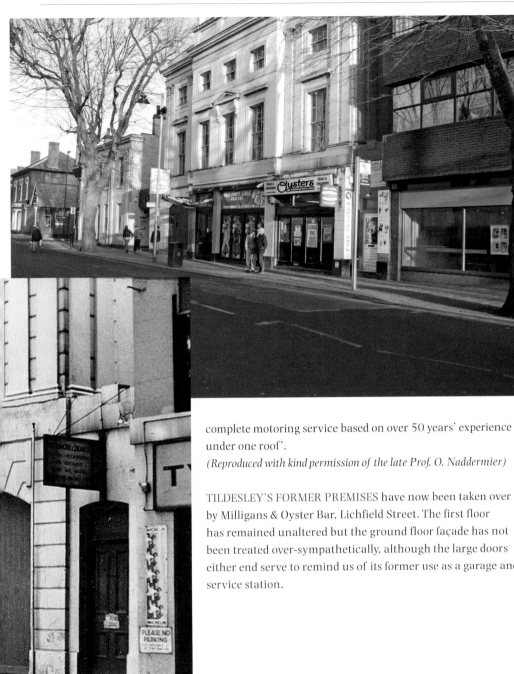

complete motoring service based on over 50 years' experience under one roof'.
(Reproduced with kind permission of the late Prof. O. Naddermier)

TILDESLEY'S FORMER PREMISES have now been taken over by Milligans & Oyster Bar, Lichfield Street. The first floor has remained unaltered but the ground floor façade has not been treated over-sympathetically, although the large doors either end serve to remind us of its former use as a garage and service station.

ADDISON COOPER'S, LICHFIELD STREET

WESLEYAN & GENERAL ASSURANCE Society offices in the late 1960s and Addison Cooper's pillared porch two doors away is an attractive scene, with the natural brick façades and windows with glazing bars. This stretch of Lichfield Street had originally consisted of well-to-do detached houses, which in recent times have been converted to offices, although in some cases new purpose-build ones, such as the Health Authority, have been constructed.

(Reproduced with kind permission of the late Prof. O. Naddermier)

ADDISON O'HARE'S SOLICITORS' office remains relatively unaltered, although the local authority has planted shady trees along the pavement. Some of the alterations in the former Wesleyan & General building have been less sympathetic. Peter Pyne's hairdresser's sports a blue plaque to artist, photographer and local historian Billy Meikle (1858-1943).

THE HEALTH AUTHORITY, LICHFIELD STREET

THIS SHOWS THE next section of Lichfield Street stretching from Addison Cooper's to Pritchard Cycles. This group of fine, converted domestic houses and

offices on the edge of the town centre has suffered some change in recent years, as shown in the next picture.

(Reproduced with kind permission of the late Prof. O. Naddermier)

THIS SCENE IS now Lichfield Street from the Health Authority offices to those of Bradin-Trubshaw, solicitors. On the left of the picture is the Health Authority and next to it is Crooke's office, which was built originally by Jackson the Builders as their head office with a joinery shop to the rear, hence the initials in the gable 'BJK'.

BROADWAY NORTH

THIS SHOWS A circus parade, led by one of their elephants in Broadway North in 1950, probably on their way to the Arboretum. Such occurrences were almost annual at one period. This is a section of the ring road and there are proposals to widen and improve this part of

The Broadway as it emerges from a brand-new junction at the foot of the hill.
(Reproduced with kind permission of R.A. Brevitt)

THE SAME PART of Broadway North now. The elephants have gone as well as the children. For some years the Walsall Metropolitan Borough Council has refused to allow circuses that use performing animals. The tree in the front garden is now but a stump, although the glazing bars in the house remain unaltered.

ST GEORGE'S CHURCH

ST GEORGE'S CHURCH, near the junction of Persehouse Street and Walhouse Road, designed by Robert Griffiths of Stafford in a Geometrical style, was built 1873-5. A tower and spire were intended but never built. It was demolished in 1964 as its congregation had shrunk and the building was very dilapidated and becoming dangerous.
(Reproduced with kind permission of K. Rock)

WALHOUSE CLOSE, WALHOUSE Road and Persehouse
Street are built on the site of the former St George's church,
whose interior was highly decorated. The pillars were of
York stone. The low walling in the picture is formed from
the lower courses of the stone wall formerly surrounding
the church.

MELLISH ROAD CHURCH

MELLISH ROAD METHODIST church in a picture postcard in its heyday. This had been a particularly popular church and contained some impressive stained-glass windows, which were salvaged when the church became redundant. Since the early twentieth century it had stood as a landmark at the northern gateway into Walsall at the end of Mellish Road.
(Reproduced with kind permission of the late Dr C. Hollingsworth)

MELLISH ROAD METHODIST church has been redundant for twenty years. It is a Grade II listed building and, although damaged by some subsidence, it was to be restored and proposed to be used as a homoeopathic centre. Regrettably, the latest proposals are, with the approval of English Heritage and Walsall MBC, that it is to be demolished and the site developed.

MOSS CLOSE

MOSS CLOSE SCHOOL, the long front, taken on 11 February 1963. For some years this had housed the Queen Mary's Grammar School Preparatory Department and the first year of main school.

When the new buildings were ready in Sutton Road, this became redundant and was eventually demolished. *(Reproduced with kind permission of the late R.A. Stone)*

THE HOUSES OF Moss Close, which have replaced the Queen Mary's Grammar School Preparatory Department. The grammar school, which was founded in 1554, had been on a number of sites before it moved into the purpose-built school on Lichfield Street in 1850. When the Queen Mary's Grammar School for Boys moved to Sutton Road in 1965, the Queen Mary's Girls' High School expanded into the building in Lichfield Street. In 2005 the buildings were listed Grade II.

SAVOY CINEMA

A PICTURE POSTCARD of the Savoy cinema, 1938. This was the first project for R.G. Madeley in 1936 when he joined the local practice which became Hickton, Madeley & Partners. The film *The Joy of Living* was made by RKO in 1938, starring Irene Dunn and Douglas Fairbanks Junior. *(Reproduced with kind permission of the late J.S. Webb)*

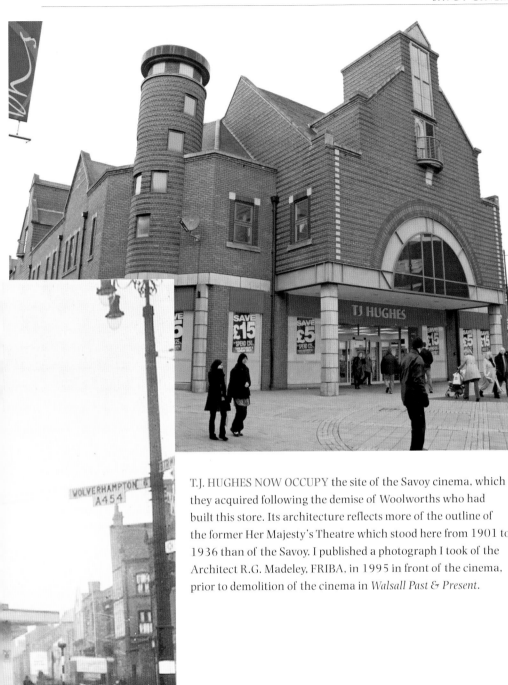

T.J. HUGHES NOW OCCUPY the site of the Savoy cinema, which
they acquired following the demise of Woolworths who had
built this store. Its architecture reflects more of the outline of
the former Her Majesty's Theatre which stood here from 1901 to
1936 than of the Savoy. I published a photograph I took of the
Architect R.G. Madeley, FRIBA, in 1995 in front of the cinema,
prior to demolition of the cinema in *Walsall Past & Present*.

PARK STREET

THIS IS THE top of Park Street in 1965. This picture suggests that some of the buildings were due for replacement by this time. It was open to two-way traffic in those days and had been part of the route for buses, trams and, later, trolleybuses. Nowadays, it is completely pedestrianised and the lower end even hosts some market stalls.
(Reproduced with kind permission of D.J. Payne)

THIS CURRENT VIEW of the top of Park Street shows how well the new paving and street furniture, such as the street lamps and seats, fit in with Park Place, which had originally been named the Quaser Centre. Park Street takes its name from being the road to the ancient park full of deer and good timber, which lay to the west of the town and was first mentioned in 1247 as belonging to the Lord of the Manor, William Rufus.

PARK STREET STATION

HRH PRINCESS MARGARET at the station, 1 May 1951.
The station clock stands at five to two. Ahead of her the
princess had a busy schedule: dedicating the Walsall
Memorial Gardens, presenting new colours to the Sea
Cadets and visiting W.R. Wheway's chain works.
(Reproduced with kind permission of R.A. Brevitt)

THE PARK STREET station entrance is now through the
Saddlers Centre next to Marks & Spencer. On the opposite
side of the street, next to a new Macdonald's stands the
Priory Inn, which has been restored, then W.H. Smith
housed in a former Birmingham Dairy's building, both of
which do not appear much altered since 1951.

STATION STREET

THE OLD STATION entrance of 1849, Station Street, in the 1960s. This was the third station after Bescot Bridge and Bridgeman Place and was designed by former Queen Mary's Grammar

School boy, Edward Adams of Westminster, and is of a similar design to another of his stations at Lichfield. The station also closely resembles Queen Mary's High School for Girls, which he designed in 1850 as the boys' grammar school. The former South Staffordshire Railway building on this site was used as the parcels office from 1884 until the Park Street building was destroyed by fire in March 1916. At this point the Station Street building reverted to being the main entrance until the prestigious new Park Street booking hall was opened in 1923 by the newly-formed LNWR.

THE CURRENT STATION entrance, Station Street, is by no means as impressive as that of 1849 and the Station Street building in this picture provides a side exit from the platform.

HER MAJESTY'S THEATRE

THIS IS HER Majesty's Theatre of 1900 when the area was decorated to celebrate George V's Silver Jubilee on 6 May 1935. The theatre, with one of the largest stages in the country, dominated Park

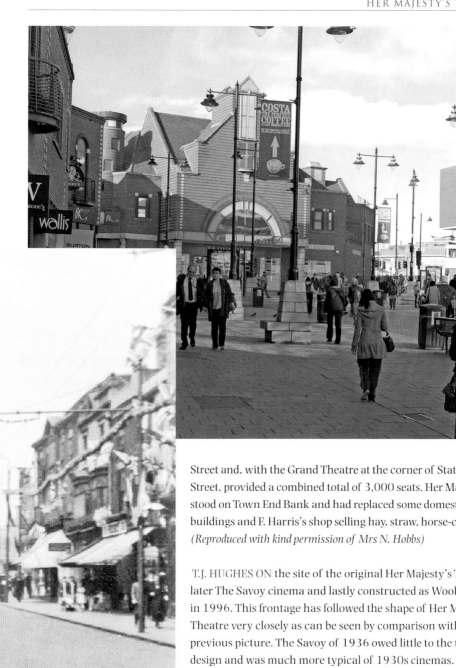

Street and, with the Grand Theatre at the corner of Station Street, provided a combined total of 3,000 seats. Her Majesty's stood on Town End Bank and had replaced some domestic buildings and F. Harris's shop selling hay, straw, horse-cut chaff. *(Reproduced with kind permission of Mrs N. Hobbs)*

T.J. HUGHES ON the site of the original Her Majesty's Theatre, later The Savoy cinema and lastly constructed as Woolworths in 1996. This frontage has followed the shape of Her Majesty's Theatre very closely as can be seen by comparison with the previous picture. The Savoy of 1936 owed little to the theatre design and was much more typical of 1930s cinemas.

PARK STREET FROM THE BRIDGE

PARK STREET FROM The Bridge in May 1935, with the bunting displayed for George V's Silver Jubilee. Two-way vehicular traffic is evident, but the mist has rendered the two theatres in Park Street invisible, although the street is clean and relatively free of traffic. *(Reproduced with kind permission of Mrs N. Hobbs)*

THIS VIEW FROM the bottom of Park Street shows a pedestrianised area with the market established at the lower end of the street. On the right is the landmark building of Lloyds TSB. The beehive logo carved in stone was chosen by Lloyds Bank by chance. When they were founded in Birmingham the event was reported in *Aris's Gazette* alongside an item about beekeeping with this illustration. In the distance, the square top of the New Art Gallery Walsall can just be seen.

THE RED LION

THE RED LION was preserved in the midst of the new buildings constructed towards the end of the 1990s. This side of Park Street used to be home to The Grand Theatre, until it was destroyed by fire just before the outbreak of war in 1939, at the corner of Station Street at the

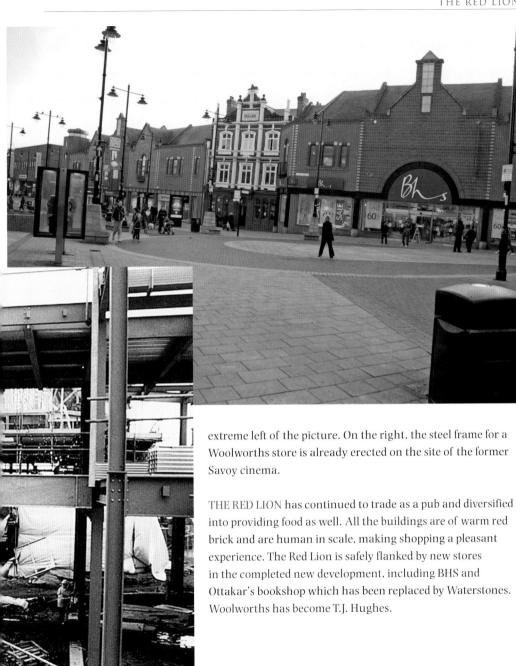

extreme left of the picture. On the right, the steel frame for a Woolworths store is already erected on the site of the former Savoy cinema.

THE RED LION has continued to trade as a pub and diversified into providing food as well. All the buildings are of warm red brick and are human in scale, making shopping a pleasant experience. The Red Lion is safely flanked by new stores in the completed new development, including BHS and Ottakar's bookshop which has been replaced by Waterstones. Woolworths has become T.J. Hughes.

BRADFORD PLACE BUS STATION

BRADFORD PLACE IN the 1960s. This view was taken from the rooftop and shows the buses in the foreground with a refreshment vehicle for bus crews at the right-hand side. This area was

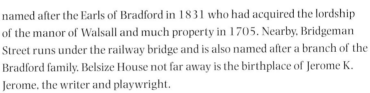

named after the Earls of Bradford in 1831 who had acquired the lordship of the manor of Walsall and much property in 1705. Nearby, Bridgeman Street runs under the railway bridge and is also named after a branch of the Bradford family. Belsize House not far away is the birthplace of Jerome K. Jerome, the writer and playwright.
(Reproduced with kind permission of D.J. Payne)

BRADFORD PLACE BUS station, showing that the refreshment vehicle has gone and so have the Midland Road railway sheds in the background. The Cenotaph stands here because it is on the site of a very large bomb crater resulting from a Zeppelin raid in 1916, during which Mrs Slater, the mayor, received fatal injuries from flying glass while on a tram. On the right, the coat of arms on the building is that of the Saddlers' Livery Company and decorates Saddlers Centre shopping mall. The tall bronze pinnacle appearing from behind the market stall is a 'nombelisk', which carries the names of families recorded as living in Walsall.

BRADFORD PLACE

BRADFORD PLACE IN 1965 shows the former range of shops culminating on the left in Ratners the jewellers on the corner of Park Street. As you can see from the road-markings, through traffic was then able to travel across The Bridge and along Lichfield Street or up Park Street. The buildings on the left are apparently post-war and not very inspired architecturally.
(Reproduced with kind permission of D.J. Payne)

BRADFORD PLACE ON the right is a purpose-built shopping arcade with steel and iron framing exposed dating from 1897. Visitors have likened it to New Orleans. Inside there are two malls

known as the Victorian Arcade with glazed barrel roofs. Traffic has now gone from this part of Bradford Street since 1963, apart from buses and taxis. On the left it is possible to see how the market stalls have encroached from The Bridge area.

BRADFORD PLACE FROM THE RACECOURSE

BRADFORD PLACE FROM the site of the former racecourse, based on a drawing of 1840, which was tinted in 1913 by thirteen-year-old Master H. Stone, a pupil from the school located in the building with the portico in the centre of the long block on the right.

(Reproduced with kind permission of the late R.A. Stone)

TO TAKE A picture from the same viewpoint is no longer possible. This is because supermarkets are what you see from the site of the former racecourse. It is possible, however, to get a good view of Bradford Street from Midland Road. The portico in the centre led into a school in 1913 but it now leads into a business management college. The far right end of the block is Belsize House, the birthplace of J. K. Jerome, which has recently received a blue plaque from the Jerome K. Jerome Society. His most famous work was *Three Men in a Boat*.

LOWER HALL LANE

JUST BEHIND BELSIZE House, at the junction of Lower Hall Lane with Caldmore Road and opposite The Vine, now a non-alcoholic public house and drop-in centre especially for young people, the end building was, in 1952, Roebuck's general store. In addition to being a

neighbourhood general store, the owners also used to sell ice cream at the market in the nearby High Street and Digbeth quarter of the town.
(Reproduced with kind permission of R.A. Brevitt)

IN LOWER HALL Lane the Roebuck's general store has been replaced by an office block, which used to house the Social Services Department and has now been renamed Millenium House, a base for Peopleserve, which helps people train for work. Behind it lies the site of Shannon's Mill, which was destined to be converted into a shopping centre with accommodation above but suffered total destruction in a fire.

THE GENERAL
(SISTER DORA) HOSPITAL

THE GENERAL (SISTER DORA) Hospital in the late nineteenth century. This hospital was the inspiration of Sister Dora and was opened in 1878, the year she died, but she was too ill to

attend the ceremony. It has now been demolished, apart from the former nurses' home, which is divided into flats. The site has been developed by a partnership between Accord and Caldmore Area Housing Associations. An Edward VII pillar box still stands on the right-hand corner.

ACCORD AND CALDMORE Area Housing Association dwellings on the site of the former General (Sister Dora) Hospital, at the junction between Vicarage Place and Wednesbury Road. These dwellings are in a good elevated position, just out of the town centre and within easy reach of shops. They are also well placed to reach exit roads to the M6.

WEDNESBURY ROAD CONGREGATIONAL CHURCH

THERE WAS A very damaging bomb raid across the West Midlands by a German Zeppelin airship at the beginning of 1916 and Walsall, along with Tipton, was hit. This shows some of the Zeppelin bomb damage at the front of the former Wednesbury Road Congregational church, which was eventually demolished in 1973. No-one was injured at the church, but Mrs Julia Slater, the mayor, was a passenger in a tram along the road in Bradford Place and was injured fatally.
(Reproduced with kind permission of Mrs M. Ward)

THE ZEPPLIN RAID of January 1916 resulted in a stick of bombs landing on Wednesbury Road and Bradford Place. The Wednesbury Road Congregational church was very badly damaged at the time. It had been designed by Jerome K. Jerome's father, an architect and cleric from Appledore in north Devon who had had differences with the Congregational church in Bridge Street, Walsall, and established a church on Wednesbury Road in protest. The Glebe Centre has replaced the Wednesbury Road Congregational church, while the congregation has joined the Broadway United Reformed Church.

DARLASTON ROAD

TRAM NO. 40 at the generating station in Darlaston Road in 1892. Despite being numbered '40', this was in fact Walsall's first electric tram. The first tramways had opened in December 1884 and were electrified later. All services operated from a terminal on The Bridge from 1901 until, on 30 September 1933, the last tramcar ran to Bloxwich. The first trolleybus service had already opened in 1931.
(Reproduced with kind permission of P. Abbott)

TWO TICKS WINE warehouse bought out Whittalls Wines, Darlaston Road, and now occupies not only the former South Staffordshire Tramways Electric Generating Station, but also the former Partridge Steelworks. The South Staffordshire Tramways established this generating station in 1892 and had situated it next to the Walsall Canal, which was used to deliver coal to the steam-driven generators.

FELLOWS PARK

SCHOOL CHILDREN GIVING dance displays in front of a large crowd as part of the Coronation celebrations of 1953 at Walsall Saddlers' former ground, Fellows Park. Until 1930 the ground was known as Hillary Street and then was named after H.L. Fellows, a director of the club. Their biggest

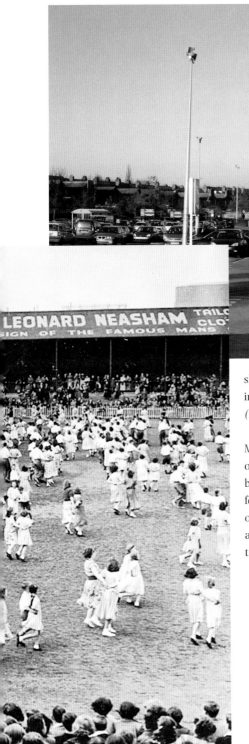

shock result was when they beat Arsenal in the Cup Final in 1933.
(Reproduced with kind permission of R.A. Brevitt)

MORRISONS SUPERMARKET, WALLOWS Lane, occupies the former Fellows Park football ground. In the background it is possible to see tunnel-back housing still featuring as it did in the days of the Walsall Saddlers' occupation of the site. Walsall Football Club occupies a new stadium at Bescot on the site of a former sewage treatment works.

THE ELMS

THE ELMS IN Sutton Road, pictured in 1953, was at one time a private house where Dr K. Anderson ran her surgery. During the Second World War it was the Home Guard headquarters, and in this photograph it was being used by the Territorial Army. Harry Glaze's coach is from the firm he ran in Stafford Street.
(Reproduced with kind permission of R.A. Brevitt)

GORDON HOUSE TERRITORIAL Army Centre stands on the site of The Elms. It is now the base for Territorial Army members of the Royal Engineers and for the local Army Cadets. During the Fire Service strike Gordon House acted as a station for the Civil Defence fire appliances, nicknamed the 'Green Goddesses'. These Bedford vehicles were built between 1953 and 1956 for the Auxiliary Fire Service and, after the AFS was disbanded in 1968, were mothballed only to be used during Fire Service strikes. They have all now been sold off or scrapped.

BROOKHOUSE FARM

BROOKHOUSE FARM HOUSE in 1952, just prior to demolition to make way for a private housing estate. Brookhouse Road, built in the 1930s, was named after the farm to which it was adjacent. The actual site of the farmhouse is, however, in the post-war housing estate of Gillity, which takes its name from a farmhouse, 'Gillity Greaves', originally located at the end of Allington Close. Greaves Avenue takes its name from it too and means 'woods'.
(Reproduced with kind permission of R.A. Brevitt)

ELIZABETH ROAD LEADING to Gillity Avenue runs across the site of the former Brookhouse Farm. There were 65 acres belonging to it when William Reynolds farmed it in the 1870s, having been publican at the Wheatsheaf, Birmingham Street, for a time. He eventually moved to the 40-acre Broad Field Farm near the former Malt Shovel.

PARK HALL

PARK HALL IN 1950, just before demolition, was one of the last large houses to go. It was a little run down in 1939 but survived as an officers' mess for the duration of the Second World War. It had been a fine house architecturally, and even the door furniture was of high quality, including silken panels. *(Reproduced with kind permission of R.A. Brevitt)*

PARK HALL SCHOOLS now stand on the site of the Park Hall house. The Park Hall Infants' School has 322 pupils and is regarded as outstanding following Ofsted's inspection.

The junior school has 400 pupils and the Park Hall Community Association is based here too. Their mission statement says: 'Park Hall Community Association strives to listen and act upon the requirements of the local community, helping them to help themselves fulfil their lifetime aspirations by providing educational, social and recreational opportunities.'

GRANGE FARM, SUTTON ROAD

GRANGE FARM, SUTTON Road, 1953, was owned by the local authority and farmed by tenants such as the Reece family, largely as a dairy farm. Mr Reece used to wear an old smock and deliver

milk to householders. The local authority created a rear entrance into the Arboretum extension at this point off Sutton Road and laid out a small car park. The site of the farmhouse eventually passed into private ownership and a detached domestic house was built on it.
(Reproduced with kind permission of R.A. Brevitt)

141 SUTTON ROAD, which has recently been considerably extended, stands on the site of the Grange Farmhouse in the previous picture. In 1937 cricket and football pitches were laid out on the former Grange Farm. In 1951 a former pavilion was converted to a theatre and became known as the Grange Playhouse and is currently Walsall's only live theatre.

Other titles published by The History Press

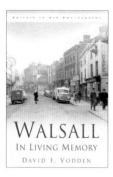

Walsall in Living Memory
DAVID F. VODDEN

This is a superb collection of over 200 photographs selected and informatively captioned by David Vodden. *Walsall in Living Memory* contains pictures from the author's own and other private sources, many of which have never been published before. It is sure to bring back happy memories to those who know the town, as well as providing a valuable insight into its part for visitors and new residents alike.

978 0 7509 4322 2

Walsall FC Images
GEOFF ALLMAN

Walsall Football Club have never payed in the old First Division and have never graced the Premiership, yet this Midlands club has warmed the hearts of the nation with their giant-killing feats and plucky promotion campaigns.

With expert captions from experienced soccer writer and life-long fan Geoff Allman, this superb pictorial history will appeal to fans of all ages as an evocative journey down memory lane or a glimpse into the way things used to be.

978 0 7524 2091 2

Haunted Black Country
PHILIP SOLOMON

From Brierley Hill to Walsall, Netherton to Darlaston, this chilling collection of true-life tales covers the whole of the Black Country. Many of these tales have never before appeared in print. Compiled by the *Wolverhampton Express & Star*'s own psychic agony uncle, Philip Solomon, it contains a terrifying range of apparitions, from poltergeists and ghosts to ancient spirits, silent spectres, haunted buildings and historical horrors. This comprehensive collection will delight anyone with an interest in the darker side of the area's history.

978 0 7524 4882 4

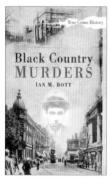

Black Country Murders
IAN M. BOTT

The Black Country is a distinctive industrial region, formed by centuries of mining and iron forging. Here evolved a breed of people accustomed to the darker tragedies of life, often witness to horrific scenes in industrial catastrophes, and home to some of the most gruesome murder cases in Britain's history. In this book are the stories behind some of the most heinous crimes ever committed in the Black Country. Ian M. Bott re-examines the cases, most untold or unpublished since they were first sensationalised in newspapers contemporary to their time, in this must read book for true crime enthusiasts everywhere.

978 0 7509 5053 4

Visit our website and discover thousands of other History Press books.

www.thehistorypress.co.uk